I GOT THE

KEYS!!!

Michael Lavan

Copyright © Michael Lavan, 2018

The author reserves all the right to this book. They do not permit anyone to reproduce or transmit any part of this book through any means or form be it electronic or mechanical. No one also has the right to store the information herein in a retrieval system, neither do they have the right to photocopy, record copies, scan parts of this document, etc., without the proper written permission of the publisher or author.

Disclaimer

All the information in this book is to be used for informational and educational purposes only. The author will not account in any way for any results that stem from the use of the contents herein. While conscious and creative attempts have been made to ensure that all information provided herein is as accurate and useful as possible, the author is not legally bound to be responsible for any damage caused by the accuracy as well as use/misuse of this information.

Acknowledgment

First and foremost, I thank God for giving me the ability to have a successful real estate career. For giving me the courage to leave another full-time job to pursue real estate and for giving me the experiences I have had so far that will enable me to pass all these information to you.

I thank all those who will be buying this book and also those that have always supported me in my real estate career. Thank you for taking the chance on reading this book. I hope you get to learn a lot from it.

I thank my family who is always supporting me. To my wife, Jackie, thank you, I love you. To my daughter, Amara, thank you for helping me organize this book and put together this book. To my second daughter, Jasmine, you've been amazing.

Also, thank you to my mentor Rosalie and my office manager, John, who has primarily been the one giving me all the information of what I know about real estate. I did not learn these from a book; it's been the majority of his experience when I ask questions. Thank you for being there for me and being supportive enough to answer every question that I have had.

And lastly, I say thank you to myself; for believing in myself and not setting any limits to how far I can go or how much achievements I can make in this world. For feeling confident enough to put together a book to share information with the world.

Contents

Acknowledgment

CHAPTER ONE

    Learn From My Tale 1

CHAPTER TWO

    Client-Agent Relationships 13

CHAPTER THREE

    Why Should People Buy Rather Than Rent? 22

CHAPTER FOUR

    No Window Shopping. 26

CHAPTER FIVE

    Team Work Makes the Dream Work 31

CHAPTER SIX

    Shop Until You Drop 37

CHAPTER SEVEN

    I Got The Keys 43

CHAPTER ONE

Learn From My Tale

Is it not true that if you are 24 years old, working for a state job where you have a pension, benefits, a good salary with overtime included, that you would pretty much be set in your career? And that in such beautiful days of your lifetime, you will be so comfortable with the secure bright future ahead that leaving such a job will be considered the most insane decision? Well in my case, that wasn't it at all. I found myself being in a place for 8 years where I wasn't thrilled, and I'd reached my full potential.

I tried to figure what the next step was going to be, and I honestly had no answers, until one day I was put into a position where I couldn't go to work for a couple of months. And being outside of work, and only bringing home a regular paycheck without the overtime wasn't cutting it. At that point and time, I had to find myself a second job to compensate for the overtime I missed. I went to a place that sold watches, and during the interview, I told the manager I didn't want to do sales, I just wanted to do stock. She said, "No problem, you're hired."

So, the real turning point came as early as the second day! I had to confront the thing I hated most - sales. This was what happened. The store got really busy, and they asked me to come out on the sales floor- which I was apparently not too happy about, but being the team player that I am, I quickly made up my mind to do my best, in spite of my feelings towards aspects of business relating to sales. As I ran the sales floor, I realized that I'd went ahead and sold 4 watches within the first hour or two, which was kind of unheard of at that time. And at that point, I realized sales was something I could do. It was a natural thing for me: it was easy for me to connect with people- people honestly felt comfortable doing business with me. So, from then on, I always wanted to do sales- I wanted to be the best at what I did. What was erstwhile a much-hated thing became my beloved and opened my eyes to new vistas of opportunity and expanded my heart to see beyond the limits I had set for myself. Sales, in other words, became a springboard for the other great things that happened in my business life after that day.

When it came to different competitions in the store, I was all for it. Then my mother actually gave me the idea of getting into real estate. It was really not one of the things on my mind at that moment because I really didn't know much about it. In other to make the most of my mother's advice, I went to my local office and just sat down with the manager to get information. As I was sitting there, she slid me a fake commission check, which showed what one average wholesale in the area goes for- what I could make. And the numbers on that check off of selling one house was what got me interested! It was one of those mind-boggling sums that one finds within his reach, as long as the necessary efforts are applied.

You could guess that I straight away made up my mind to take a real estate course online. The course was very long, and a very stressful process. And truth be told, the best friend to online courses is procrastination - at least from my own experience. What I noticed myself doing was taking the course online and recognizing that real estate was about a bunch of policies and rule while not really teaching you how to sell houses.

As time went on, and my life started to change for the better, I got called back into my regular job. At that point, and in consideration of my position, I really couldn't stand going to that place, so I knew I had to make a change.

I dedicated a lot of my time at that job to studying my real estate course, preparing myself to take the real estate exam. A couple of months passed, and I continued my studying, completed the course, and had to take my real estate exam.

This was an exhilarating moment in my life. Writing an exam whose course content you found boring... yet important, gives birth to a collage of feelings. At one end of it, you know you need to pass it at all cost. On the other hand, you are not sure you will pass an exam whose content you did not find interesting and enjoyable. This was how it went: I wrote it for the first two times, and the result was an abysmal failure. And with failure comes discouragement.

Naturally, I was discouraged... I was distraught. I thank God for my wife who was supportive and pushed me to retake it. But for her motivation, we would not be here at this moment. She is figuratively the writer of my success story in this business. After her powerful motivation, I regained my courage. But the problem was, I felt the pressure of people knowing I was taking the exam but not knowing I could pass it.

So, one day I told my wife I was going out of town for something and snuck up to Albany, NY to take the test. I did what I did that the day to avoid the shame that comes with failing. I didn't want anybody else knowing I had failed it again if eventually, I failed.

And third time is a charm; I passed the exam. Once I passed, I went back to the local office that had given me the advice, to begin with, and I sat down for an interview to become a real estate agent. In becoming a real estate agent, I still had to do my full-time job to compensate for my income until real estate took off.

When I got into the office where I currently work my first shock was that a lot of the more experienced agents told me they didn't like dealing with rentals. It would have been detrimental to my career to allow myself to be influenced by their prejudice, so I made a firm decision to be an all-around learner. The most important thing was to learn about the field of real estate first and get comfortable showing people houses. I knew that every good thing would come with time.

I took all of their rental leads, and before you know, I was closing 2 to 3 rentals a week, which translated to easy money as you get paid faster on rentals than you do on the closing of a home.

From then on, I reached out to a couple of my closest friends and social circles to let them know I was doing real estate to see if they knew anybody that was buying or selling a home and if so, to refer me. My first deal came from a co-worker who was looking to buy a house in the local area. It was a smooth process as I already felt comfortable with him long before the deal.

So, on a given day, I went to look at houses with him and his wife, and there was this one particular house that they loved, but it already had a buyer. What I did was to reach out to the selling agent anyways to see if we could still see the house. We went to see the house, and naturally, they fell in love with it- it was everything they hoped it would be.

Since the contracts were not signed yet, I asked the agent if it was possible for us to offer more than the asking price for the home. She presented the offer to the seller, and the seller agreed to the deal. We signed contracts, and that was my first official closing. The process was great, and from there I grew, closing a couple more sales by the year's end.

From then on, I realized that real estate was something I really enjoyed doing: I loved the freedom on having an open schedule and being out in the field all day without anyone telling you when you can take a break, when you can use the restroom, or when you can use your phone.

Being in this field taught me a lot about the hustle and bustle, but also taught me the appreciation of opportunities. As I was still carrying my other full-time job for the state, I was not allowed to bring my cell phone inside the building and recognized that I was missing a lot of business. There would be times when I would go to my phone on break, and there would be 6 or 7 missed calls from potential clients, and by the time I called them back, they already had different agents. With clients/customers being the lifeline of every business, I know you could fully gauge my rage at missing such great opportunities. Sometimes, it feels like feeling sorry for yourself for not being at the center of the great things happening in your life. But, at the same time, it offered me the highest drive to make the urgent and vital decision I needed to make at that moment in life.

As time went on and I continued to grow in this business, I realized I had to make the big decision once and for all: I could stay at the job I worked 8 years at but had already peaked in and was no longer happy at, or I could try a new field that is considered risky to some. Can I trust the power of my hard work and dedication to the level of financial success I have always dreamed of, or I should content myself with my current lot in life? This and many other questions were what I had to mull over a thousand times.

I thought hard about it. I talked to my parents about it, talked to my in-laws about it, talked to my wife about it, and I prayed on it. And with all those people around me, supporting the decision I had to make, I decided to resign from my full-time job and pursue real estate full time! This was the d-moment of my life.

In the beginning, it feels like going nude! While hopes are high, you just can't keep the fear away!

At the point- the end of 2016- I became Regional Rookie of the Year and Regional Top Sales Agent at my agency. With the help of my mentor, I realized real estate was a great business as long as you worked hard, dedicated yourself to your clients, and most importantly making sure you find the home they like and being consistent in what you say and what you do.

My career took off after my first year, leading into a great second year. People were noticing who I am, and what I'm doing, and how I can help them as far as buying or selling their home. With the help of social media marketing and the marketing that my company offered, I became a real household name in the area as far as real estate agents and started getting a lot of other referrals from people who were looking to buy or sell a home in the area.

I kept pushing and realized a lot of times buyers were struggling with the process of being a first-time homebuyer. As I grew my business, I started to learn more things about it, which was very helpful. Being knowledgeable in my field helped me show my clients the easiest and best ways to make smooth transactions. My role in their lives could be summarized in one word: fulfillment.

Which is why I'm here now: to share with all of you the step-by-step process of buying the home of your dreams. That home that will bring you the fulfillment that comes with owning a home of your own. I guess you love it!

CHAPTER TWO

Client-Agent Relationships

Relationships are everything in this business. While this may be said about life, it seems that the realities of this are more dramatic and evident in businesses like real estate, where the joys or anguish that come with a single transaction may last a lifetime. It's crucial as a real estate agent to have good relationships with a strong team around you. When I say team, I mean inspectors, attorneys, mortgage lenders, contractors, and so on. This is crucial because when you come across a new client, especially a first-time home buyer, you want to able to fulfill whatever needs or obligations they may ask of you- but we'll get into that further down the line.

The most important relationship is that of the agent and the client. Find yourself an agent that you are comfortable with- almost as though you're building a friendship with. Find someone you'd love to have come by for your housewarming party - someone you'd want to show your friends and family. In other words, a relationship that holds the texture of eternity.

For agents: No pen, no matter how mighty, can imprint the sublime feelings that come with knowing that you helped somebody achieve something they will forever be grateful for.

I advise clients to develop the right habits that are required for having the ideal agent. When out and looking for agents, create habits like looking up their Zillow reviews- if an agent doesn't have a Zillow account at this point and time in their career, just make sure they are knowledgeable and thriving in the business as most top agents do have a Zillow Account.

Read their reviews, reach out and see if you can contact some of their previous clients to find out about the work ethics that each agent possesses. You want to make sure that no matter what happens, the agent that you sign with is an individual that can address whatever needs you may have.

So, do your homework on an agent before you decide to dedicate your business to one. And kindly make sure this agent can fulfill your needs as a client. It's one thing to open doors and have buyers walk around, and another for an agent to show you the homes, explain the pros and cons, talk to you about the area, the location, the school district, and more to help you feel comfortable that that home is fit for you. And in cases where such dwellings may not satisfy your needs, to help you with data that will lead to making an informed decision.

Make sure you and your agent have excellent communication. You want to find someone who can provide information, when you have questions, in a responsive and well-educated manner. It is evident that as a first-time buyer, you will have a lot of questions. The agent who provides the best answers to the varieties of questions that crop up at every stage of the transaction has clearly proven himself/herself worthy of doing business with.

This is a big investment. Probably, the biggest investment you'll ever have. You'll hear me say it multiple times- you're not buying a pair of sneakers, you're not buying new clothes, you're not even buying a new car. You are buying a home, so you want to make sure that your relationship and communication with your agent is prompt and accurate.

Be alert! You don't want an agent that doesn't really know what they're talking about and misleads you with the information they gave. You don't want to find out once you've purchased the property and are locked into a thirty-year mortgage. This will be a lifetime mistake you don't want to ever make. So, let your right to correct information be the first to assert in this investment.

Another important factor when picking out your agent is "comfort." Whether you're going about this process with a significant other or on your own, you want to make sure that you are around someone that you feel comfortable with. Remember: you're going into vacant homes with this individual, so it's always necessary that you feel comfortable with your agent. Trust me, I've never heard of any horror stories with real estate agents and their clients, but you always want to make sure that you're safe in all aspects. The comfort you get from the person you are around with takes care of the stress that comes with moving from one vacant home to another.

Recognize that there will be points in time when your realtor is not available because as real estate agents- although this is our line of work and our business- we also do have personal lives ourselves and families we need to maintain too. Real estate agents wish they give all of their time to clients, but the natural order of things require you give to every aspect of life its due right.

Don't be discouraged if you reach out to your agent now and then and (s)he is not available. But do make sure that you have an understanding with your agent that if they're not available, it's OK, but to please make sure they get back to you. As realtors we sometimes, find ourselves staying away from our phones for 2 or 3 hours at a family function, or with other clients, and then once we get back to our phones, we have often had a bunch of text messages, voicemails, or emails we need to get back to.

Understand that we as realtors will try our best to get back to you, and no matter what happens, our primary goal is to reach out to you. So, if you find yourself with the realtor that's not responding or getting back to you, this is a red flag. Unresponsiveness is tantamount to bad business ethics, and there are no ways around this. There are specific points and times where there are deadlines for putting in offers. If you want to edit your last offer or to put in an offer to begin, you won't be able to partake in the bidding process and could even lose the perfect home due to a realtor that couldn't submit your offer in a timely fashion. Time is key! Let there be consciousness of time at every stage of the transaction. This is one way to ensure the best deals are not lost due to negligence.

You want to make sure you give your realtor the respect of their own personal time, but without sacrificing the timely service you need from them.

Have fun with your realtor. This can be a stressful process or a fun process. Make sure to find yourself a realtor who makes things as positive and enjoyable as possible. Positivity matters most at this stage in life. It provides the boost you need to confidently navigate all the challenges that come with this investment Go out there, point out certain things about a house that seem awkward and laugh at it. Point out other things about a house that may look nice and appreciate it. Let there be positivity and laugher when the situation demands it.

You might walk into a house that looks like a train ran through it, you might walk into fantastic and beautiful homes, either way, take something positive away from the process and enjoy it with your realtor.

Realtors see hundreds of houses a year. We may even see a house multiple times with different clients, so we know certain things about the home- sometimes even before we walk through the door.

Everybody's eye is different. As a client, you may like quality in a house that someone else might not. So, when you enter a home, it's with fresh eyes. At such moments. It is certain that you'll notice what you like and what you don't. And that's fine as long as you enjoy the process the whole time, and you enjoy the company you've chosen to include in this journey. Make it a positive experience. You never want to feel like you're just stressed out the whole time, and that house hunting is haunting. This could be a serious source of discouragement. And if it turns out this way, it leads to frustration for the realtor because it means as realtors, we're not doing our job.

Can it be stressful for clients? Yes.

Can it be stressful for realtors? Of course.

But the most important thing is to get to our common goal: the closing table.

CHAPTER THREE

Why Should People Buy Rather Than Rent?

A lot of time people don't even realize that they're ready to purchase a home.

They are just so used to renting out apartments or single-family homes that it becomes an automatic process in their lives. It becomes easy for them that they fail to realize that if they could spend a little bit more (or even a little bit less) then what they're already paying in rent could end up buying a house! Sometimes, it takes too long for people realize that they the proper steps to transition from the renter's market to the homeowner's market.

This may be something as far as saving more money, increasing your credit, or getting a better income- and once you complete these steps, you are ready to get into that buyer's market. You may find that what you're paying in rent will be the same monthly payment that you can make in a mortgage. Many of those in the rental market often have the same concerns: *the space is too small. I don't like the area. I hate my landlord. I want to do renovations, but I can't.*

We've all been there- and it's at times like this that you need to realize that it's time to purchase your home. This discomforts that grow into murmurs are the best triggers you need to take that firm decision. So, make that crucial decision on where you live and how you live. Are you the type of person that wants to open a kitchen to a beautiful open concept? Do you want to paint your bedroom walls with a particular color? Do you want to change your bathroom? Do you want to finish your basement? These are the kinds of freedom you possess once you own your own home.

Other times, people come across difficult landlords. For example, things keep breaking in the house, but you can never get through to them, and suddenly you find yourself living with a broken toilet. Or the heat isn't working. Or the stove- and you end up going out of your own pocket to get it fixed because you want to make liveable conditions.

It's understandable- but it's also definitely a statement to your inner being that it might be time for you to jump into the buyer's market, or at least sit down with a mortgage lender and see what your possibilities are. At least you need to know how far you are from getting into the buyer's market even if it's out for the time being. No adult should die without a home or at least in the process of trying to own one.

It all comes down to one word: **decision**. Decide that it's time for you to be able to enjoy your own home- to make your own choices like getting that man cave you've always wanted or put up a fence, so you can finally get a pet. There are a thousand and one points of creativity and innovation that come with owning your own house. You only need to have one before you know what it means.

When you own your property, you get the freedom not only to renovate and decorate, but it also makes it easier to host events at your home. It's a hassle to organize a family barbeque when you're living in an apartment- but when you own that property? You can also have all the people you want, laughing, playing games, listening to music, doing whatever you please- your property, your rules.

CHAPTER FOUR

No Window Shopping.

Have you ever gone to the store just to look at stuff and you don't know if you can afford it? The same goes for house hunting. Some people just want to look out houses without knowing if they can afford one. What happens, in the long run, is that you see a home you love, and because you are not pre-approved with your funds to afford the house, you get stuck. You get stuck because every other house you look at does not meet your expectations like this one house. And then you feel disappointed.

To avoid this, do not window shop. Be sure you have enough money at hand before you start scouting for a house. Be preapproved before you even start looking at houses.

This is a significant factor because:

1. It gives you the idea of the types and ranges of houses you should be shopping within.
2. It saves you a lot of time going to look at too many houses that are not within the means of your financial standing. That is, scouting for homes that you're not even sure if you will be able to put an offer on any of them.

So, it is better that you stick with your lender's advice. A lot of realtors can refer some to you if necessary. Or you can sit down with your local bank and discuss what your financial options are in purchasing a home. You should consider what amount of money you can shop within to determine the kind of houses to look at.

A lot of lenders have different techniques, but most of the time, they will be able to tell you what your purchase price for a house will be as well as the taxes you should be looking to pay because a couple of thousands of dollars in your tax amount could significantly change your mortgage plan. So, it is essential you sit with your lender or bank to check your financial standings to determine the price range of houses you should be looking at. They will check your credit, income, etc. These are parameters you need to monitor well from about 6-9 months out before you purchase a property. You want to ensure your finances are in good standings before you go for your pre-approval, and it's after this you can know the best course of action to take and decisions to make.

At the point of the buying process, there's a trick I use for buyers, and that is to give them a reverse action. Figure out what is comfortable for them to be paying on a month to month basis. For example, if you're comfortable paying $1700 a month including your mortgage and taxes, make sure you inform your lender of that and then ask what purchase prices you should be looking at that will give you that monthly focus. A lender could then tell you that they would pre-approve you for say a house worth about $250,000 with $6000 in taxes. And this is what will give you the monthly installment you want. It's better to do that way because the worst thing a person wants to do is to get their first monthly mortgage to be paid and then it's far more than they ever bargained for.

I tell all my buyers, "Do not buy a house to work just to pay for a house. You should be able to own a beautiful home and enjoy it. Have big barbeques and vacations. All these stuff factors into your lifestyle while owning your home."

And this is why it is essential to make sure that you set a comfortable budget on paying a monthly mortgage. Tell your lender the figure so they can tell you the price range of houses you should be shopping for while wanting to purchase a home.

CHAPTER FIVE

Team Work Makes the Dream Work

Now that you got your number squared away regarding the price point you should be shopping when you want to purchase your home; it is a crucial step to find a good Realtor who's going to help you find that dream house you've been looking for. Finding a good realtor could be done in so many ways: you could call different offices, you could look on google to see any realtor reviews, what house they have sold and what areas they've been selling homes, etc.

You definitely want to weigh out all your options and do your research when finding that perfect realtor because you want to make sure that you're working with someone who's able to provide the information or answer the questions you may have before even considering putting a person in a home.

Keys to Finding a Good Realtor

When finding a good realtor, there are certain things you want to look out for.

- Is the realtor part time or full time? There's nothing wrong with being a part-time realtor. As we all know, some of us may have other jobs and responsibilities, real estate may be a second job which is okay, but the thing with a part-time realtor is you are going to get a part-time extension. You may call them with your questions, but they might not be able to answer or get to you right away. They may be unable to attend to your concerns and needs in a timely fashion because they do have other obligations. However, with the full-time realtor who makes real estate their 9 to 5 jobs (or for some of us make our working hours 9 to 9), they are prone to be more responsive and reactive to what you need. You may call them, and even if they do not answer, you know they're working with other clients or doing other work. Text message and email are other effective methods to communicate in this business as well.

- You also want to find that realtor who knows the market you're looking into. If you're looking at homes in a particular town or area, you want to have someone who has some experience with real estate in that area. That is, someone who can tell you about the school districts; who can tell you about the local shopping or activities that the town has to offer; the distance of the nearest highway if you choose to commute to work or family; among other factors being considered. So, you definitely want to have someone who's experienced in the particular area or district you're looking at so that they will give you the detailed information you may not find online.

- It is also good to have a realtor who's experienced enough in the business to know what to look for in houses. Sometimes, walking through homes, you may not pick up on certain things that realtors will pick up on. And this will save you the time and energy of putting an offering or to pay for a home inspection that will later turn out bad. You want to consider this because as realtors, we inspect homes on a daily basis and see the good, the bad and the ugly. So, trust that we can prevent you from purchasing something that has the ugly involved in it, we can easily spot aberrations with a property including those things you consider as reasonable. We immediately know if it's not an excellent location or a good home for you to live in.
- A good real estate agent can also tell you certain things about what kind of pre-qualification you have in what to look for in a house. If you're a

FHA qualified buyer, and then you see a home you like but may have appraiser issues such as water damage or cheap paint, we will tell you right away, "Hey, we understand you like this house but understand that there will be issues that the seller would need to address if we have appraiser command here and it's not guaranteed that the seller would want to address it."

So, we make sure you're looking at homes that don't have these issues and concerns so that when we get to that point down the line, it wouldn't be a bad thing for an appraiser to come near and see certain things without us being worried about it.

Those are all the things you want to find in your agent because they will be the one that will basically break down to you the location you want to buy in, what the neighborhood has to offer, the kind of home you should look at and what the house has to offer as well and make sure that all four of these things are in place so that when you do make your decision, you will be one happy buyer.

CHAPTER SIX

Shop Until You Drop

So, you have decided to buy your dream house. You have now been preapproved, and you've spoken with your realtor. Now that you're preapproved, it means you actually have the amount you need to buy a house or shop within. Now, you're ready to shop for your home.

You can think in two ways when shopping for a home; that is, figure out if it'll be for short term or long term. Some people try to consider their status to determine how much space they need and for how long they would be in the house, i.e., if or not they are married or have kids. As a single guy or lady looking for a home, and with no kids, the short-term option is what you'll most likely want to opt for.

Irrespective of whether you're shopping for short-term, you still want to put in the same effort and go through the same process you will if searching for long-term to ensure that you get what's suitable for you. But you might not want to explore too much before settling for an option since you're only getting the house for a short period. It could just be a condo townhouse as you don't need anything too big. Most of these are location specific as it's not everywhere you find smaller homes as compared to family houses that you can see everywhere.

If you're thinking of a long-term search like for 30 years until you pay off your mortgage, that's also a great idea. You could get this to build a happy family around friendly neighbors and making them grow with other kids in the same neighboring school and all. Getting this kind of house involves the same process as well.

Regardless of what option you decide to go for, your considerations should be pretty much generic. You want to make sure you shop for home options that are comfortable for you financially, have a good school district, with reasodnable taxes, as well as proximity to your work depending on where you work.

A lot of first time home buyers will usually put together what I call a "wish list." And that is good as most realtors will wish you have these needs and wants to have an idea of what you have in mind. I always say to buyers, "You will find things that you need in a house, and you'll also see things that you want in a house. But you should understand that it's most important to consider getting what needs and be sure to have the potential of turning it into what you want."

That's a big step because a lot of times, buyers are always looking for granite counter tops, Stainless Steel appliances, Recess lightening, the finished mancave basement, master bathroom, the walk-in closet, the pool in the backyard, etc. While these are all fantastic features to have in a house, but you need to be sure your price point will actually get you a house that has all these things. Usually, a home with all these things will be quite costly, but if you get a house that doesn't have these, you can always tweak in some of these things later on especially if you have space.

Understand that *potential* is an essential factor to consider when shopping for a home especially if you do not have the financial means to afford a fully furnished apartment. Get what you need and pay a reasonable price for it now, then later fix in the things that you want since it has the potential for space. Always keep that in mind – always consider potential when shopping for a home.

When you're out with your realtor searching for houses, you want to ask questions like, "How's the school district?" "How's the noise? Is it quiet by night?" "Is it busy during the day? Is there a lot of traffic in this area? Where are the local shopping areas? Are there local restaurants? How's the job availability in the area? Where are the local highways"?

These are questions you want to ask your agent because you don't want to be in for any surprises after moving into the area only to discover some aberrations you weren't aware of. I personally feel that the more questions you ask, the better. Asking many questions shows that you're actually interested in that particular property, so the realtor will ensure to answer all as adequately as possible.

If you do find that property you see potential in, ask these questions and more to prevent surprises after you have received those keys. As realtors, we are here to serve you; we are here to make sure that this process is as smooth and enjoyable as possible. As I said earlier, you are not buying a shoe; you are not even buying a car. You are buying a home, and it would be the biggest investment of your life. You need to make sure that you are confident and delighted with what you're buying. The worst thing that can happen to a buyer is to purchase a property and then 2 years later; you're back on the market looking again because you didn't get to enjoy the one you initially bought.

As a real estate agent, I always tell my client, "Make sure this is the home that you love. Once you walk through that door, you would know; you would most likely feel those butterflies of excitement that confirms to you that this is what you want."

Use this to know if you love a home as well. It has worked almost all the time for my buyers; I see no reason why it wouldn't work for you.

CHAPTER SEVEN

I Got The Keys

Having decided that you want to buy a house, gone through the steps of finding a great agent to help you purchase the house, gotten a mortgage preapproval to fund your home, and inspected your chosen home to be sure it's in good condition; you are finally at the point we call *the closing table*.

This is when you sit back and start packing your boxes, start picking out designs for your bedrooms, furniture, living room, etc. And you start making your plans for probably 10 years in your new home. This is where the normal butterfly feelings of excitement of how your expected experience come in. However, this stage is also accompanied by a lot of nervousness, so it's a big step.

It's nothing that you're used to. This is your first time buying a house, and even though it's considered growth, it's a step that is about to change your lifestyle, and it's only natural that you are nervous. You might even feel that you're making a wrong decision, it's all part of the process and you need not worry too much about how you feel at this point.

Understand that at the closing table, you will be signing a lot of paperwork. Do not be in a rush, listen to what your attorney says and ask questions if you have them, and make sure you fully understand what you're signing. Once you sit down to sign all that paperwork and completed the funding requirements, then you'll have your keys. That's the magical moment; the opening and beginning of a brand-new Amazon chapter of your life. You are finally a homeowner.

You are about to start experiencing what it means to be a landlord, having neighbors who will sit outside of their wall greeting you, the kids running around, etc. You don't have to ask for permission to do stuff around your house; you have a nice big backyard where you can host family barbeques. You can now start watching your situation and family grow into an establishment and take that next step to what you consider happiness when you first decided that you wanted to purchase a home.

I am pretty sure your lender and attorney are happy for you. So, take pictures, frame these pictures so you can remember this day because this is the day many have dreamt about for years before it finally happened.

Now the time is here; appreciate the moment because you have now GOT THE KEYS.

www.ingramcontent.com/pod-product-compliance
Lightning Source LLC
Chambersburg PA
CBHW071439220526
45469CB00004B/1595